To All
With

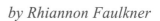

by Rhiannon Faulkner

To All Healers, With Love from a Healer

Published by Sakayi Publishing in 2008
Copyright Rhiannon Faulkner. *All rights*
reserved.Rhiannon Faulkner has asserted her right to be
identified as author of this work in accordance with the
Copywright, Designs and Patents Act 1988.

ISBN: 0-9551902-1-5   978-0-9551902-1-6

I would like to thank all my guides for giving me the opportunity to work with them.
Especially my Dr C as I call him, who asked me to channel his words for this book.
These words of wisdom, love and help are channelled directly from my spirit doctor. He wanted this book to be written as a support and guide for healers worldwide.
I would like to dedicate this book to all the wonderful healers I have met through my shop.

Love and Light

Rhiannon xx

To All Healers, With Love from a Healer

To All Healers,
With Love From A Healer.

Introduction

Giving Reiki each day in my shop and teaching students each month, it is safe to say I am passionate about healing.

I truly believe it is a gift that everybody has and one that everybody is entitled to receive. What a wonderful world it would be if we could all either self heal or know of someone to go to instead of queuing up at the doctor's surgery.

I have been told that I am different in my way of healing. Maybe this is because I don't preach about traditional methods, but focus on how healing can fit in to the modern world. I don't have time to meditate everyday as the old fashioned way teaches, as I have five children who seem to take up a lot of my time! I am a normal mother who has a very busy lifestyle. Don't get me wrong, I do meditate, just not everyday.

People come to my shop and say that they have been drawn to me for some reason, but aren't sure why. I can see the shock in their faces when they meet me and realize that I am a human being, not a witch. I like a drink, a smoke too, I am afraid to say, and sometimes I even use foul language! Some say I am a breath of fresh air as I do not look down my nose at them claiming to be a holy one !

One day, whilst giving a normal healing session in my shop, an amazing thing happened that would change the way I did my Reiki forever.

A lady came to me for Reiki as she thought it would help with her skin condition. She had a friend who was a Reiki healer and had recommended me. She was quite dubious at first but willing to give it a go.

I started off as always at the top of the head, tuning in to receiving the energy and 'feeling' how it felt to be tapped into her energy.
I came to the face and was amazed at how I could actually feel the Reiki only go through the three layers of her skin. I was actually seeing in

my mind's eye the third layer and realised that, that was where healing was needed.

The lady commented at how it felt as if she was sat under a heat lamp and I was reassuring her that the energy only went to where it was needed.

I get really excited and can't hide it, as there is no one more amazed than I when it comes to Reiki! Sometimes it is like I am standing back watching the energy at work and it fascinates me to this day.

I became aware that I had to go to her stomach. She didn't understand why, as there was nothing wrong. I kept being pulled to one side of her lower abdomen and 'saw ' a baby. I asked her if she wanted children and she replied " Absolutely not!" She didn't have any and she didn't want any either. I couldn't make the idea of a baby go away but my confidence was knocked as she had disregarded the idea immediately.

I then felt as if I was about to have one of the biggest periods ever and I told her this. She said that was strange as she was meant to have her period a while back but it hadn't happened. I knew the Reiki was working and I warned her that she would probably bleed heavily within the next few days. She left pleased with the Reiki saying it was an incredible experience, especially with the clairvoyant messages I had been passing onto her.

A few days later she came back into the shop and asked for another session. She would not tell me anything else but said she couldn't wait to see what I had to say this time. I was a bit bemused to see that her skin wasn't completely better so started off the treatment again. Instantly I was drawn to her stomach, bypassed her skin problem on the face and concentrated on the abdomen again. I was in the same spot as the first session and could feel the energy working well.

With that I was suddenly aware of a Chinese man holding a black doctor's bag, wearing a black polo neck jumper and putting on a white overcoat. He stood on the other side of the couch and he did not look at me or acknowledge me at all.

I was in utter shock and trying to keep it from showing on my face. I watched this man cut her stomach with a scalpel in a cross shape and then start to dig inside her body with his bare hands.

At this point the lady started to say that it was actually beginning to hurt. Mild panic started to kick in and I heard myself reassuring the both of us that Reiki could do no harm over and over again.

In my professional manner I could not help say something on the lines of "Oh my God, if you could see what I see!!" I ended up giving a running commentary of what I was seeing. In some weird way I thought this would reassure her that there was reason for her feeling some discomfort.

He pulled out a lump that looked like an egg; a hard-boiled one that was rubbery. He threw it away, stitched her stomach up and walked through the wall.

The lady then started laughing and explained why she had come back to me so soon. A few days after the first treatment she had had with me, sure enough she had a miscarriage. She didn't even know she was pregnant and she was taken to the hospital where they diagnosed it. They scanned her stomach to make sure it had all gone, in case she needed a DNC. This is where they had discovered the egg shaped lump in her womb.

Well, I don't know who was more shocked, me or her, we both started to laugh and said wouldn't it be funny if the lump had gone the next time she went for a scan.

She came back a few days later and said that sure enough the lump had disappeared but now she had another problem. The NHS staff were panicking at the fact that they had lost the lump. She was not brave enough to say that a pregnant Reiki healer had said that a dead Chinese doctor had cut her open and pulled the lump out! She had to go back for another internal examination and she was begging me to stop her bleeding fast to make sure that she didn't have to have the internal done.

I thought this was amazing, proof that what I saw happen was real. I decided that I would simply call him back. I started calling him in my head with no avail, I didn't give up and eventually I saw him at the end of a very long hospital corridor.

He was wearing the black polo neck jumper again but no white coat. He stared at me, almost cross that I had contacted him. I didn't have a chance to speak to him, he looked at me and said, "What do you expect?" and turned and walked away from me.

I actually felt embarrassed at disturbing this man and explained to the client that the job was done. There was nothing else for this doctor to do. He had removed the lump and that was it.

I carried on giving Reiki to the stomach to stop the bleeding and I knew it was just a matter of days before it would stop by itself.

That was my first experience of my Chinese doctor. Since that day, he has appeared on many occasions but only when physical healing is needed. He never speaks to me or even acknowledges me when at work. I just watch in amazement at what he does. It is like being a nurse in theatre, watching the surgeons at their work. He has come to assist with abscesses; pregnancies, growths, cancers and a whole lot more.

Thanks to him, I have seen inside people's bodies and watched in awe as he works. I never was very good at biology at school and don't know the names of all the parts of the body I am seeing being dissected, cleaned out or replaced - but I am learning fast!

My Chinese doctor was put hard to work one day, giving physical healing to four patients one after the other. After the last one had gone, he hung around to talk to me.

I walked into the back room to flick the switch on the kettle, and he followed me in. This was the first time I had seen him when not working! I looked at him and smiled and said thank you for the wonderful work he had done that morning. He leant on the kitchen work surface and put his head in his hands.

He was, to put it bluntly, shocked at the state of some people we had worked on. Many of them were healers themselves, who didn't have the first idea how they could heal themselves. Many healers have said to me that they believe their illness to be part of the course, or a hazard that comes with the job.

He gave me the title of this book and told me to start typing for him. I have channelled his words exactly as he said them at the beginning of each chapter- so they are straight from the doctor's mouth. I could also do with listening to him myself and sometimes I feel that he is scolding me too.

To All Healers, With Love from a Healer

CONTENTS

CHAPTER 1	MEETING OTHER HEALERS
CHAPTER 2	LETTING YOUR WORK TAKE OVER YOUR LIFE
CHAPTER 3	LIVING A GOOD LIFE
CHAPTER 4	GROUNDING AND PROTECTION
CHAPTER 5	SELF HEALING
CHAPTER 6	WHAT ARE WE CHANNELLING?
CHAPTER 7	CHAKRAS
CHAPTER 8	CLEANING THE CHAKRAS
CHAPTER 9	GET TO KNOW YOUR PARTNERS

CHAPTER 10   COMBINING
CRYSTALS WITH
HEALING

CHAPTER 11   KNOWING THE
HUMAN BODY

CHAPTER 12   PSYCHIC SURGERY

CHAPTER 13   REMOVE THE EGO

CHAPTER 14   REMOVING
NEGATIVE ENERGY

CHAPTER 15   TEACHING REIKI

CHAPTER 16   WHY CAN'T WE HEAL
EVERYBODY?

Chapter 1

Meeting other healers

First of all, let's remember one thing. There is no competition as to who is the best healer or who works the best way. Respect each human being whom you meet and consider the path that they are on is completely different from yours. Honour each other's way of working and only give advice if you are worried that they are not working through light.

Wise words I say. The amount of frosty healers I meet in my shop is laughable. Surely we should be glad to meet like- minded people. But no, so many of us seem to be threatened by other healers or other forms of healing. Don't be concerned at what level they are or what qualification they have, be grateful for meeting someone else who might understand your path.

The feelings of competition, not being as good as the other healer, less experienced, more experienced, threatened - all show that you have a dent somewhere in your aura or your belief in your own healing abilities.

Listen to other healer's experiences, enjoy sharing stories and respect their way because it is right for them and your way is right for you.

Always remember that your guides are with you for a reason and their guides are with them for a reason. We all have work to do and we should be working towards the same goal.

I have heard many people boast about their healing abilities and proclaim that their way is best. I have heard many people ask what level or standard another Reiki healer is, before they will even consult them regarding a health problem.

I have seen many spiritual healers slate Reiki and claim that their way is the one true path. I have spoken to Reiki healers, who will not accept clairvoyant healers and vow that it is wrong to pass on the messages whilst healing. Yet I believe that I get the messages not for me but for the client and sometimes a comforting message from a deceased loved one or words of encouragement from a guide is all the healing that person needs. This upsets some healers and makes them steer clear of me as I frighten them. Remember - each to their own!

Clubbing together with fellow healers is a wonderful idea to help each other every now and then. Who heals the healer? There is this myth that all healers are automatically well all the time as they have non-stop access to this energy. Making time to work together with a group of healers is really worthwhile, taking time to give healing to each other. Swapping notes and stories can also give you a boost - encouragement that you are not on your own and that you are doing a good job.

To All Healers, With Love from a Healer

Chapter 2

Letting your work take over your life

We do not expect your bodies to be on hand every minute of every day. We come when needed and act upon your request. You have every right to say no and must practise this often. If you allow yourself to be open to receive, then we will assume you are in a position to work. Strict guidelines for your routine in life must be in order at all times.

We seem to think that because we have this ability we must use it at all times. If you could see what you look like as a healer the way I see you, it is incredible. Imagine yourself as a bright golden ball of light almost flashing like a beacon calling out to the world. It is like you are walking around with a sign over your head that says, " I CAN HELP YOU!" People are drawn to us. This is great if we are in control of it and can say the word " NO " or " Let's get the diary and see when I can fit you in ".

So often I myself come across people who need healing either on a physical or emotional level and I instantly offer my services. I genuinely want to help.

I don't think about my other commitments such as my five children, my husband and my health amongst other things. I hear myself tell my family that they don't realise how lucky they are to be healthy and do not have the problems that my clients have. I explain to my family that these people need me more than anyone right now and I have to go and help them. However one day, will I have a family to come back to? Or will they have given up on waiting for super mummy / wife?

The following poem is one that my husband wrote for me on my birthday. It made me realise that I need to divide work and home life equally and fairly.

Rhiannon

She's in demand, from a large band

For Tarot, Spiritual help or just a helping hand

Her visions and her fortunes told

Bring many to her amazing fold

She teaches the powers of good inside

And takes all knock backs in her stride

She believes in and cares for all her friends

And will always help them to no end

But to us she gives much more in life

She is an amazing loving mummy and wife

Feedback from customers is very satisfying and I think essential. However, we must leave it to dedicated times in our lives. Don't invite clients to be able to call upon you at anytime of day or night. Be strict and keep your private life private. Think of it this way - how would you be able to contact a solicitor or counsellor out of hours?

I have had several cases where client's problems really concern me. I can't switch off after they have gone, to be honest I feel so sorry for them that I just want to help. I have seen it all - homeless people, suicidal tendencies, domestic violence victims. It upsets me and I worry about them. We have to realise that we can't help everybody. I can't bring them home with me; I can't keep my phone next to my bed all night.

It's a harsh truth but how many of them would care if I weren't there the next day? How long would it take them before they found another person to take my place?

Clients can become completely reliant on you and genuinely think that it is only you who has the answer to their problem. They will have been drawn to your energy and if you have done your job properly they will feel much better after seeing you. Don't let them drain you, stick to arranged times that do not invade into your private time. We need to allocate a certain time for healing and stick to it.

To All Healers, With Love from a Healer

Chapter 3

Living a good life

Know that your life's actions reflect your soul's making. Be good, honest and loving at all times. Treat others how you would like to be treated and never walk in the shadows of darkness. Do not poison your body with bad thoughts or release them through your actions. Be kind, gentle, and compassionate and show others the way to be.

Nobody is perfect and nobody expects us to be. We are still human beings and can be wicked at times!

I like a drink, sometimes more than a few. I like to smoke and I kid myself that it is the only pleasure I have to myself. However I never mix this with Reiki.

Your body is a channel for the energy to work through - fill it with alcohol and you will have devastating results. Mentioning no names, one customer was frightened of receiving Reiki as she had had it once before and it had made her physically sick. I couldn't understand this and wondered what on earth had gone wrong , until I heard that the Reiki practitioner had been drinking red wine whilst deciding to try out some Reiki to prove how effective it could be.

Remembering the Reiki principles in our lives can help us become better people all round.
They are not just for working with - they can really make a difference in our everyday life too.
Here are some examples for you to try.

JUST FOR TODAY - I WILL NOT WORRY

Writing down the things that we worry about and actually admitting them to ourselves can really help take away some of the stress in our lives.

Write your own list and see if they are seriously worth worrying about.

My list is endless with things like : Will there be enough money to pay the bills this month - Will my car pass it's MOT - Have I done a good enough job - Will my children love me - What do people think of me.

Now write yours:

Well, I think the answer to all of your worries is quite simply ask your guides for assistance and trust that they will help you.

It tells us in the bible that God helps those who help themselves. We can't just sit and wait for life to be good - we have to at least put some effort in from our part.

So how about doing the best job we can in life, giving everything we do our maximum input and then asking our guides to make sure the outcome is okay.

A little example of everyday help that I get from my guides is that I was opening a café in my angel shop the following morning and I had 24 hours to get it ready and stocked up. I was panicking as I had lost my childcare and was really struggling with working and looking after a baby at the same time. I had done the hour-long school run that morning and had the baby with me in the car on the way to the wholesalers.

I asked my guides to stop the feelings of anxiety and to help me get everything done that I needed to before I had to pick up the kids at the end of school time. I arrived at the wholesalers, opened up an account with just a business card screwed up in the back of my purse and did my shopping.

I thought nothing of it, but thanked my guides for keeping me focused and de-stressed and I managed to get the café open in time for the next morning.

A week later, my husband wanted to open his own account at the same wholesalers so we set off on a Sunday with all five children. I assured him it was a piece of cake getting an account as I had done it myself. I told him to take a business card with him and that that was all he would need. He didn't believe me as he had tried before and needed lots of proof of identity etc. I just laughed at him.

Well, sure enough there was no way on earth the cashiers were going to let him open an account without all the relevant forms. I explained that I had opened an account only the week before with just a business card and they were, to put it mildly, shocked, saying it was not possible. As I was shouting in defence of my husband, I quickly realised how much my guides had helped me in my hour of need that day. I smiled to myself and thanked them again in my head.

<u>JUST FOR TODAY - I WILL NOT BE ANGRY</u>

Wow, this is a hard one for me. How many times do you feel yourself about to explode at the smallest of things? Next door's dog fouling on your side of the garden, other people's kids being rude, someone nicking your parking space, OLD PEOPLE PARKING IN THE MOTHER AND TODDLER PARKING SPACE!!! This list could go on and on for me personally, you can probably guess this is the hardest exercise for me!

Anger eats away at your body, making you ill from the inside out. It is important to let your feelings out. Anger is not something to be embarrassed about, but you have to learn to control it. Many people, who come from an unhappy childhood, vow never to argue in front of their children. But doesn't this lead to more problems? Maybe the children won't learn how to express their own anger.

The throat and heart chakras really do become blocked with anger. The hardest types to remove with healing are the ones that have been stored up for years and years. The healer's eye can see this as black sharp shapes, firmly rooted in the body.

So, let's list all the things that make you angry in life. Sometimes, quite simply writing them down can help us to see how unnecessary they are.

My list includes: Family, neighbours, timewasters, council tax.........

Now look at your list and see if there are any you can laugh at yourself, or others, which you can pass on to your guides and sincerely ask them for their help with this matter.

Just for one day, you are going to try and forget your anger regarding this situation.

<u>JUST FOR TODAY - I WILL GIVE THANKS FOR MY BLESSINGS</u>

It is so easy to only think of how hard done by we are, or how upset we are at certain things that have happened in a day. This list makes you realise that life isn't all that bad and makes you concentrate on how lucky you are. Sometimes we realise that things we take for granted all too easily, are the same things of which other people can only dream.

My list includes, my children, my husband, having a job I love……..

Now, the hardest list so far for me, is definitely this next one. Here we have to write down all the difficult things that have happened that have made us learn some valuable emotional lessons. We need to see what we got out of these experiences and give thanks for getting through them.

My list includes:
My divorce - for teaching me
that I can be independent and
cope alone.
Being broke - for teaching me
that money isn't everything and

how to appreciate the more
important things in life that
money can't buy.

JUST FOR TODAY - I WILL DO MY WORK HONESTLY

Admit it, how many times have you accepted the wrong change in your favour at the supermarket? Oh, come on I can't be the only one? Okay then, how many of you have accepted a parking ticket with time left on it from another shopper, saving you from having to buy one yourself? Same thing !

On this list you have to write the areas of your life where you could possibly be more honest - cutting corners in your work, pulling a sicky but being well enough to visit a friend - adding more P&P onto your ebay items....

My list includes.... Some things that I would rather not print!!

JUST FOR TODAY - I WILL BE KIND TO MY NEIGHBOUR AND EVERY LIVING THING

Mmmm, squashed a spider recently or rinsed him down the plughole? That is just as bad as kicking the dog. Shouted at your children, just because you were tired or ratty? Moaned at your neighbour because their tree was leaning over your fence? This list could be interesting, remember you only have to try and amend these things one day at a time!

My list includes,
Giving my husband the silent treatment just because I have had a bad day and he hasn't.
Swatting flying creatures in my house.
Forgetting to feed the rabbit as it was raining and I couldn't be bothered to go outside.

Well done for admitting these problems out loud. That was step one. Now just pick one Reiki principle for today and give it your best shot.

Nobody expects us to be perfect, it is enough that we try. Buddhist monks get to meditate on each one of these every day. We don't, however, as our lives are so busy with so many commitments.

Just carrying one of these principles with us for a day can really make a difference. The "I will not be angry" one is great for when going on a long car journey - it can help with the odd bout of road rage!

To All Healers, With Love from a Healer

Chapter 4

Grounding and Protection

You need to be focused on your intentions to heal other people and protected from their emotions and diseases. The golden rule is so often forgotten and devastating results can be had. Take time to nurture yourself before and after a treatment. We do not expect you to be affected in any way, physically, emotionally or mentally.

Grounding and protection are not always taught within Reiki and I strongly feel they should be.

Before you begin giving Reiki you need to ground yourself. Grounding is a way of making you concentrate on the here and now and on what you are doing. Once you are fully grounded or rooted you may actually feel heavier and more alert. It stops your mind wandering onto your Tesco shopping list or the next client's problems etc.

Protection is needed every single time too. You are tapping into your client's emotional problems; depressions, fears, anxieties and memories or life's scars. You do not want to take them on yourself.

You can easily protect yourself by imagining a bubble around your entire body, a bit like a washing up liquid bubble, or a hamster ball! Only good can come through your bubble and all negative energy bounces off.

Some people talk of cloaking themselves for protection. They imagine a purple cloak wrapped around them to keep them safe and protected, or a wall of mirrors around them to send the negative energy back to where it came from. However, I personally disagree with the mirrors idea as I would never want to harm anyone - not even if they intended to harm me originally.

I have had great problems grounding in the past. You will only find out how necessary it is to be grounded and protected by not doing it just once. You will feel almost as if you are floating out of your body or get the terrible shakes due to the strong amount of energy running through you. After each Reiki session, you, the healer should be left feeling energised and refreshed or buzzing. If you feel drained or exhausted then you have not grounded yourself well enough. Your client will leave feeling great - but you have taken on how they first felt when they came to see you.

Grounding yourself can be done in 5 minutes if not seconds when you get the hang of it. I now do it when I first meet people or bump into people unexpectedly, like mothers in a playground that I don't know just in case they have any negative energy around them. Think about how you feel after a friend phones to tell you about her problems - she feels better for offloading and you feel drained and depressed just by listening to her on the other end of the phone. Protect yourself at all times, you are there to listen, not to take on their emotions.

Here is a simple grounding process that with a bit of practise can be done in five minutes, or is perfect for a full relaxing meditation when you have the time.

Sit down with your feet uncrossed and flat on the floor. You can lay down with your knees bent so again your feet are flat on the floor.

Close your eyes, and concentrate on your breathing becoming regular and deep.

Imagine roots of an oak tree growing from the soles of your feet. Make them thick ones pushing through the floor. Imagine them getting longer and longer, thicker and thicker. See new roots growing off the sides of the large roots, again growing longer and longer.

See them forcing their way through the foundations of the house, creeping through the cracks in-between the concrete. They are now becoming longer and longer, stronger and stronger, working their way through the earth, wrapping themselves around huge boulders deep down in the earth.

Force these roots all the way to the centre of the earth, where you can see a huge golden ball of light.

With each breath in, you are drawing this light up through the roots you have planted.

See the light travel all the way up the roots slowly. Continue breathing in deeply and bring the light all the way up through your feet. See and feel the light start to travel up through your shins, through the knees, through the thighs.

Keep focusing on your breathing, making sure it is deep and rhythmic. The golden light is now entering your spinal column, filling your whole torso. Feel it travel down the arms right down to the fingertips.

It travels up the neck and fills your head, finally pouring out of your crown chakra like a fountain.

Your body should feel warm and your feet heavy. You should now feel grounded, relaxed and in tune with your Higher Self.

Bubble your entire body with the transparent ball of protection.

Take time to gather your thoughts, allow your mind to wander wherever it wants to take you.

If you are short of time and you only want to ground yourself before going somewhere that needs your complete concentration, it is fine to just imagine the roots connecting with the core of the earth and no need to draw the light up through your body.

When you are finished, it is important to close down. Slowly and gently drain the light from your body, starting with the head and pushing it all the way back down to the core of the earth. Cut the roots when you have finished, but keep the ball of protection around you.

To All Healers, With Love from a Healer

Chapter 5

Self healing

Self-healing is a critical step for all of you. You need to remember you are entitled to receive just as you give to others. The damage I see that healers have allowed to happen to their own bodies saddens me. It is the lack of self worth, always wanting to be recognised as doing well for others, yet not realising your own health is at risk. Your wellbeing is our main concern, to allow us to work together you must be fit and well.

An obvious comment, yet such a common problem. This includes me I am afraid to say.

I have heard so many stories of the most incredible healers having to stop as they have worn themselves out, some have become seriously ill and had to stop work.

I have come across many healers who are ill either physically or emotionally. I have had periods where I have suffered physical symptoms of anxiety, symptoms I never understood before I had them myself.

Emotional healing, concentrating on the relevant chakras is essential on a regular basis for all of us.

If you are suffering from a problem, emotional or otherwise - do what you would do for a customer! Dig down to the root of the problem and then give healing. How come it seems to be built into a healer to only give to other people and never themselves ? Yet, we all know that a physical illness always stems from an emotional problem.

After my caesarean, I had infection after infection and it wasn't until one of my customers innocently asked why I couldn't heal myself that I took note.

That night, I lay in bed and called upon my Chinese doctor. The pain was unbearable and I kept bartering with God that I wouldn't have to go into hospital and leave my kids again.

He appeared next to the bed and quite simply said, " All you had to do was ask."
I watched in amazement as he produced some kind of syringe. I felt the pain of him inserting it into my scar. He drew out a large amount of fluid and then disappeared. It hurt so much to even move and I was getting very upset. I thanked him though and fell into a deep sleep.

The next morning my husband asked how I was feeling and I looked down at the scar. I was horrified to see a huge sack of puss on the surface. It was so full that as I stood up it tore and white fluid came gushing out. Being queasy, I panicked and thought I would have to go to the doctors again. It was my husband who stated the obvious - "Isn't that the liquid that your doctor syringed out for you last night ?"

The pain had gone, the infection had gone and I now know first hand what it feels like to have surgery from this man.

Self-healing isn't only to be done if you are ill though. Finding time to give yourself the benefits of healing is essential to keep you well in body and mind.
It also helps you relax and find time to connect with your guides. A bit of "me time" or a L'Oreal moment. (As the adverts say - because I'm worth it).

Self Healing Hand Positions

1. Over the eyes.

2. Over the cheeks, thumbs just under the ears.

3. Back of the head with the base of the skull in your palms.

4. Palms over the throat or just beneath it.

5. Hands side by side over the chest.

6. Hands side by side over the bottom of the rib cage.

7. Hands side by side at the level of the navel.

8. Hands side by side between the navel and the pelvic area.

9. Hands side by side level with the bottom of the pelvis.

10. One hand on each knee.

11. One hand on each ankle.

12. One hand on the sole of each foot.

13. Both hands on head, between the crown area and base of skull.

14. Both hands on the back of the neck at the top of the shoulders pointing towards the middle of the back.

15. Both hands on the middle of the back as high up as you can reach.

16. Both hands on the middle of the back level with the bottom of the rib cage.

17. Both hands on the lower back at the base of spine.

18. One hand on the back of each knee

19. One hand on the back of each ankle.

20. One hand on the sole of each foot.

To All Healers, With Love from a Healer

Chapter 6

What are we channelling?

Know only that it is all from the same source. Stop trying to define it, just let it work through you. Bring religion into the equation and you can start conflict. Do not try and understand it's origins, just use it for the good purposes only.

Do not try and convert other people to your way of thinking, let your work speak for itself.

I like to see it as a golden light that is working through me. I am a visual person and like to 'see' what I am doing. However, there are many different names or titles that are given to the energy.

A Light

An Energy

The Divine Light

The Creator

The Holy Spirit

The Chi

Whatever you call it, respect it and respect what others call it too.

Opening up to receive the light is essential before any treatment. After a while it can be done in seconds which is particularly useful when you need to give healing in an emergency - such as in the case of a burn or accident.

Follow this simple routine each time:

1. Ground yourself with roots

2. Surround yourself with the bubble of protection.

3. Imagine a ray of golden light from the heavens above entering the top of your head, filling your whole body.

4. Ask for guidance and protection whilst you work.

Loop yourself into the client's body with an imaginary rope in a figure of eight around your body and theirs. This enables you to feel in your own body, how they feel physically. This is a great technique so often overlooked. It helps you to understand where the pain is and how intense it is.

Closing down after treatment is just as important as opening yourself up.

1. Cut the ropes so you are no longer looped into them.
2. Say thank you to your guides for their work and let them know you are about to finish.
3. Shut off the crown chakra where the light is entering your body.
4. Cut the roots from your feet.

Follow this simple procedure every time, it will prevent you from feeling drained or taking on the persons emotions.

Customers like to fill you in on the details of their problems after the session is complete, often confiding in you with their problems. You still need to be protected and grounded whilst listening to their problems so don't close down until they have gone.

Chapter 7

Chakras

Chakras are spinning balls of energy located in different areas within the body. They keep us mentally, physically and emotionally balanced. They are our energy centres.

When a chakra is blocked or has stopped spinning and is not working properly, this is because of an emotional or physical problem in the body.

1. The Base or Root chakra is associated with the colour red. This chakra is the grounding force that allows us to connect to the earth's energies. A healthy root chakra gives us stability in life, patience courage and success. An unhealthy or blocked chakra is the cause of uncertainty, low self esteem and lack of confidence.

Physical parts of the body affected: Pelvis, Testes, Genitals and Legs.

2. The Navel chakra is associated with the colour orange or red-orange. Our passion and creativity stem from this chakra and we are full of new ideas, strength and have an inner power to succeed. Signs of a blocked navel chakra are often feeling lethargic, being tired and run down.

Physical parts of the body affected: Ovaries, Kidneys, Lower Stomach, Prostate and Spleen.

3. The Solar Plexus chakra is associated with the colour yellow. This is the area that gives us our self esteem and confidence. This intuitive chakra is where we get our gut feelings or instincts from. It signals us to do or not to do something. Strong self esteem is required for developing your psychic skills so this is an important chakra to keep healthy for all healers. This is also the chakra responsible for our sense of humour too and is like our inner glow or warmth.

Physical parts of the body affected: Digestive system, Liver, Gall Bladder.

4. The Heart chakra is associated with two colours - green and pink. This is our love centre and is often the focus of a healing session. Hurtful situations like divorce, separation, grief, abuse, abandonment and unfaithfulness or betrayal all affect this chakra deeply.

Physical illnesses brought on from hurtful situations need an emotional healing as well as the physical. Basically, we have to get to the root of the problem or reason for the physical illness. Stored up emotional pain in this chakra can cause devastating illnesses. The first step to gaining a healthy heart chakra is learning to love yourself, which is harder than loving any other person in your life.

Physical parts of the body affected: Heart, Lungs.

5. The Throat chakra is associated with the colour blue. This chakra is our will centre. To keep this chakra healthy we have to learn to express ourselves honestly. This is often harder than we think. Keeping your true feelings inside is damaging, lying and denial are too. Keeping feelings locked up inside is a common problem for polite and insecure people. In time it can have devastating effects on your health.

Physical parts of the body affected: Throat, Mouth, Thyroid glands.

6. The Third eye chakra is associated with the colour indigo. It helps us to learn from our experiences and put them into perspective. This chakra helps us to develop our intuition, vision and concentration. It is the chakra that clairvoyants and mediums use to be able to "see".
Physical parts of the body affected : Central nervous system, Ears, Nose, Sinuses, Lower brain.

7. The Crown chakra is associated with the colours white and purple. It is often seen as a lotus flower opening up to act as a connection to the energy or source we channel as healers. This chakra is like a door opening up for the energy to run through us and is therefore an important one to keep healthy and clear.

Physical parts of the body affected: Upper brain, Pineal Gland.

The colours related to the chakras can be seen whilst giving Reiki to some people. Your guides may well choose to show you colours to tell you which part of the body you need to work on. You may get flashes of a particular colour or you may see swirls of it fill the room in your minds eye. Don't be frightened, it is a fantastic way for your guides to communicate, before you actually hear their voices.

Always follow your intuition. Again, it will take time to get to know off by heart which colour relates to which chakra. And, which chakra relates to which part of the body. It will all come with plenty of practise.

Remember, the chakras relate to physical AND emotional problems.

Chapter 8

Cleaning The Chakras

Sometimes when a client comes to you for healing, all they really need from you is a chakra treatment.

If they have never experienced spiritual healing before, then they will not have even heard of chakras. The following treatment is one I use quite often for new customers.

First of all , you tune in, standing at the top of the head, opening up to receive the energy and letting it flow naturally. Become aware of how the body feels, physically and emotionally as normal.

Go down to the root chakra when you are ready as this is always the first chakra to begin with.

Scan with your hands to feel where the chakra is. You will feel a heat or intense coldness (depending on how you feel or sense energy) When you have found the exact spot, let the energy flow for a few minutes.

Without actually moving your hands, imagine in your mind that you are taking the red ball of energy out of the body and holding it up , cupped gently with both hands. Blow off any dust, polish it up until you can see it shining brightly, then gently put it back in place. See it spinning beautifully before you move onto the next chakra.

Repeat this for each chakra working your way up to finish with the crown chakra.

When you have finished all of them, stand at the top of the head and give Reiki to the whole of the body through the crown chakra. Look down the body and "see" all of the chakras like colours of a rainbow or fountain of colour bursting out of the body.

This is a wonderful way to make sure the body is working in perfect harmony and a fantastic way to introduce people to the wonderful world of Reiki. More often than not, people will leave saying they don't quite know why but they just feel better and more full of life.

It should take about 20 minutes from start to finish. You may like to do this before a full body treatment or use it as a finish to the session.

To All Healers, With Love from a Healer

Chapter 9

Get to know your partners

In order for you to realise your true potential as a healing channel, you must start to be aware of your "guides" who work through you. It is no good working blind, so to speak.

When you see for whom you are working the responsibility of the patient's expectations of a cure is taken away from you.

In simple terms - it is not you they have come to get help from, but us.

Why do you think they arrived at your door in the first place? Everything in life is being organised at a much higher level than you can see.

Speak to us and we will respond, sometimes with words, sometimes with pictures or thoughts.

We can make you listen and perform our way.

I have learnt from Rhiannon that it is sometimes important that we communicate verbally. Reassurance to you I realise.
Rhiannon has always watched me at work but I did not feel the need to speak to her. However, now I need her to communicate with paper and pen for me.
Self doubt is a barrier that stops us from doing our work. You must all have belief, intent and utter trust that we are working through you.
You each have many guides that are doing their duty via you.
Do not mistake them for your carers, they are different yet again. We are only talking about the healing guides today.
It is pointless to waste time chatting, the time to connect with them is whilst you work together. Watch and learn each time you see them. Recognise when the different

faces appear - most often for the same healing need.
One will work through you for emotional treatments and another only for physical - like me.

The need for finding out our history is yet again to confirm your own belief in what you see. Ask us for a name and we will give you one. Not always the correct one, maybe one for ease on your part.

There are many CD's on the market nowadays to help you learn to connect with your guides or angels and I recommend them wholeheartedly. Guided meditations are brilliant for people like me, who find it hard to concentrate. It stops your mind wandering onto the shopping list or hoovering that you should really be doing.

Also, sitting in a development circle to learn how to see and hear spirit is a good idea too. All spiritual churches have one, make sure you feel comfortable with the people who are running it. Choose carefully, making sure that they don't have an ego showing.

It takes a lot of time and patience to be able to connect with spirit. Start to meditate when you are on your own and with no chance of being disturbed. Remember your guides need to learn how to work with you too and need time to learn how best to connect with you. Think of it as tuning into a radio station, having to get the right frequency on both sides, so you can hear and be heard.

Becoming aware of spirit around you often starts with your sense of smell. You may smell a perfume, or flower scent, with no logical explanation of where it came from. Acknowledge it, ground and protect yourself and listen to your inner voice.

See how you feel - do you feel happy or sad? Has anyone popped into your mind suddenly? Such as a grandmother or auntie that you could associate with that smell?

As you progress, you will go through a lot of different ways of spirits trying to make themselves known to you. Ears ringing, seeing moving shadows out of the corner of your eye. This is not to scare you, this is just your psychic abilities developing slowly.

We have all had that horrible feeling of being watched or just knowing that there is someone close to you. Imagine it as spirit wanting to get your attention, not to frighten you , but to get your help. The majority of contact with spirit is because they need your help, either to pass on a message to a loved one or to move them on properly to the light.

To All Healers, With Love from a Healer

Chapter 10

Combining crystals with healing

Crystals are a natural source of the earth and have been used as powerful tools to assist all sorts of healing over the centuries. We like to see people becoming educated about the benefits of these instead of using western medicine each time a health problem is diagnosed.

I sell crystals in my shop and am fascinated by the healing powers proclaimed by many books and people. They are an amazing tool to use when healing.

There are hundreds of stones with different healing properties and many books differ, offering different ideas on how each stone can help us. My simple golden rule is pick the stone that picks you. You will find that stones just seem to stand out from the display or you are drawn to a particular one and you don't know why. It is trying to tell you something !

I do not lay stones on chakras, or use them in my healing sessions, as this says to me I am losing faith in the energy that I am channelling. But this is just my personal thought. I know that they work and that many healers have amazing results from crystal healing.

However, I do like to give a tumble stone to a customer at the end of a session to help them continue working with a particular emotional problem that they have such as confidence, worry, anger or strength etc.

To start off with, stick to the colours of the chakras. If a stone is a similar colour then relate it to that part of the body.

Root chakra - RED, ORANGE

Navel chakra - ORANGE, YELLOW

Solar plexus chakra - YELLOW, GOLD

Heart chakra - GREEN, PINK

Throat chakra - BLUE

Third Eye Chakra - VIOLET, PURPLE

Crown chakra - PURPLE, WHITE, CLEAR

Black stones such as onyx, tourmaline and hematite are great for grounding and protection. I would use these for the root chakra to keep people focused and concentrating.

Black onyx is brilliant for protecting a house or a room. (I have it hidden in the four corners of my shop). Keep them out of sight and it will stop negative energy from coming in.

Citrine is fantastic for money matters! A small piece kept in your purse will ensure it is always full and a piece in the far left hand corner of your house will keep money coming in regularly.

Rose quartz is for all matters of the heart. Great at loving others but not too great at loving yourself? Then this is the stone for you. Put it in your bra ladies - so it is close to your heart chakra. Men, this stone is brilliant for having on your office desk, to keep you calm and have compassion for those annoying customers you deal with. It basically brings peace and harmony to the office! I have a large piece on the floor in my bedroom. It seems to stop the arguments over who is going to get up and feed the baby at 2am. We now discuss it fairly and amicably!

Lapis Lazuli is my favourite stone. I associate it with the third eye chakra and use it for intuition and psychic abilities. I wear this a lot in jewellery and find it helps immensely. It can be easily confused with sodalite so make sure it has flecks of gold in it.

Clear quartz is the most powerful stone of all in my experience. It is the stone that cleanses all chakras and parts of the body. It can also be used to charge other stones. I use it to remove any serious problem from a body, such as chemicals or poisons etc. You can see how dull it goes after being used and it will obviously need cleansing straight away before it is used again. This shows me that the stone has taken the chemicals out of the body and retained them.

Another favourite of mine is Angelite or Celestite. The angel stone. It is hard to find but worth paying for when you do, either in raw or tumble stone form. It is said to draw the angels close to you and keep you safe.

Tumble stones are fantastic to keep in your pocket, but so many people I meet have large collections stashed in their handbags. This is pointless keeping them tucked away and altogether. They need to be used individually and held in the hand or kept out on display for maximum effect.

Cleansing tumble stones is vital too. They become filled with the negative emotions or energies that you bought them for in the first place. They often need to be cleansed and recharged. Put them in a bowl of water overnight on the windowsill and let the moonlight work it's magic. In the morning you will find the water has a lot of grit or dirt in the bottom of it. The stones will be ready to go and gleaming, looking refreshed.

Another quick way to cleanse stones is to hold them over the smoke of an incense stick. Let the smoke completely wrap itself around the stone for a few minutes.

Stones need cleansing as soon as you buy them and bring them home. You have to remove the energies from people who have picked them up in the shop to try them out.

I always seem to find stones and then give them to other people who I think might need them more than me. Always remember the stone belongs to the earth not you and when it is not needed anymore by you, or needed more by someone else - you will lose it. Don't worry about it, it just means that you are not meant to have it anymore. Time to find another crystal for a different purpose.

The most amazing crystal tool that I do work with a lot is my wand. I felt like a bit of an idiot at first and some of my customers looked terrified when I pointed it at them, but wow the results I have had are amazing.

The best wands to use are the ones that have been handmade and have a crystal that relates to each main chakra. Mine is about 30cms long with seven crystals along the front of it and a huge quartz crystal at each end.

During a Reiki session, when I need to concentrate on putting energy into a particular place, I point it at the area. Basically, the wand amplifies the energy running through me a hundred times over. Customers say they can feel it like a strong piercing heat. Please note these are customers who had their eyes shut and didn't know I was using it until I told them to open their eyes and look!

The first day I used my wand I had another guide appear. This one took me by surprise as he was unusual. I now call him Merlin because he looks like a wizard. He is mildly amused at his new name, but not overly keen. He is a large man, with a grey cloak and a hat just like a wizards pointy one. He is very quiet and extremely polite, always waiting until he has my full attention before he speaks. He only talks to me to tell me how to use the wand properly. He has instructed me to "flick" the wand up and down the body. As I do this, customers say it is like I am painting them with a warm liquid. All in the wrist action apparently ! As I flick it up and down the chakras, I keep my hand over the top of the head and when the wand swings up towards the crown chakra I can feel a surge of energy hit my hand each time. Try it and see what results you get!

To All Healers, With Love from a Healer

Chapter 11

Knowing the human body

Although you do not have to have any knowledge of the human body to be able to become a healer, if you want to be able to understand how you are helping someone physically, you really do need to have a basic knowledge of how the body works.

I failed my biology exam at school with flying colours, but I went on to have a great understanding of all the different systems in the body, thanks to my intensive training at beauty college. Here, we had to learn in detail about the body, bones, blood circulation, lymphatic system, digestive system, muscles, respiratory system and a whole lot more. So I am lucky I had a second chance!

If you have a common knowledge of the human body, then you will find it easier to explain to the client what you think is wrong in a particular area and why the energy is being directed to a certain area of the body. When you develop your third eye chakra and after a lot of practice, sometimes over a course of years, you will be able to see into the body. It helps if you can understand what you are actually seeing!

I like to explain to my client what is going on and when you are honoured to be working with a spirit doctor, such as my Chinese doc here, it is nice to be able to explain what you are seeing him doing. If for no other reason, but to justify the discomfort your client may be in !

I have charts on my treatment room walls of the body systems to help me - never be embarrassed to use them to clarify something you may be thinking or seeing.

The following diagrams are here to help you and hopefully you can use them as a reference.

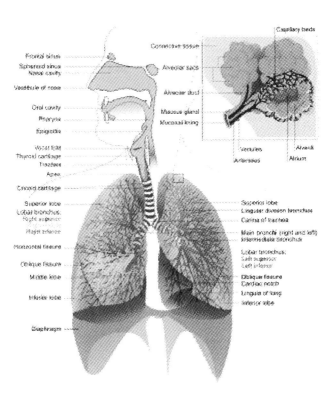

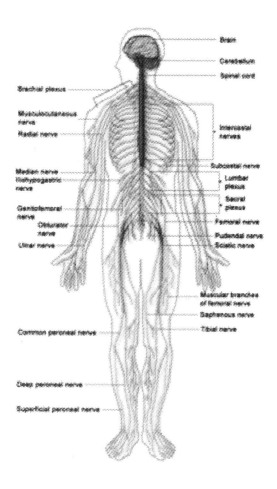

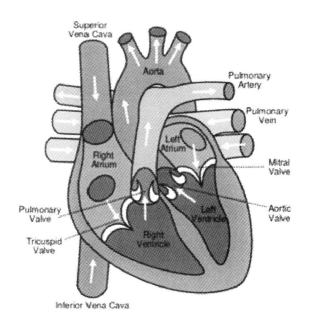

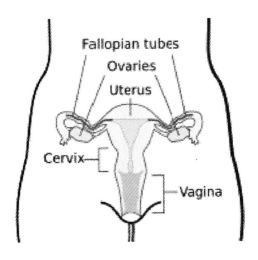

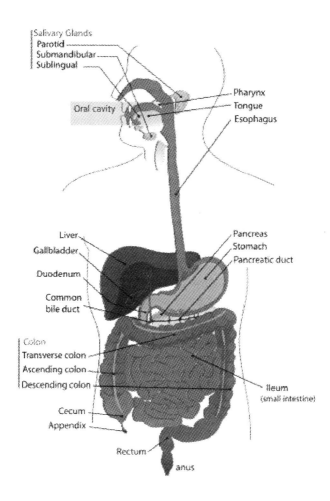

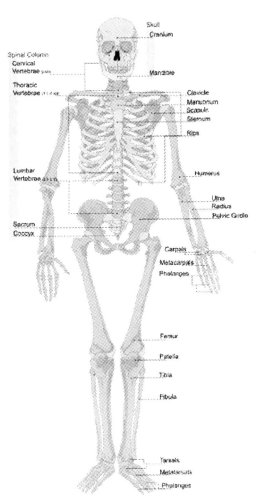

Skull
Cranium

Spinal Column
Cervical
Vertebrae (7 bones)

Mandible

Thoracic
Vertebrae (12 bones)

Clavicle
Manubrium
Scapula
Sternum

Ribs

Lumbar
Vertebrae (5 bones)

Humerus

Ulna
Radius
Pelvic Girdle

Sacrum
Coccyx

Carpals

Metacarpals

Phalanges

Femur

Patella

Tibia

Fibula

Tarsals
Metatarsals
Phalanges

Chapter 12

Psychic surgery

This is a name that westerners have given to our intensive repair work to the human body. We are surgeons who continue to practise the work we started in our lifetime on earth. Your ability to channel us comes with experience and when we feel confident you are strong enough, only then do we let you see us at work. Sometimes a helping hand from us is necessary to aid the energy you are channelling. Our intervention assists the recovery promptly.

First of all let's clear up the confusion around the words - psychic surgery.

There are gory stories associated with this kind of surgery, graphic pictures on the internet of healers hands deep down in the patients body, psychically healing or removing cancers etc.

People travel to the other side of the world to be able to get treatment from well known psychic surgeons in remote places. They pay thousands for the privilege desperate for help and more often than not come home having been conned.

I have never witnessed such healings first hand so I can not comment. What I believe is that there are a lot of fakes out there, just as there are a lot of fake psychics and clairvoyants. I also personally question why they need to go into the body if the healing they are channelling is genuine in the first place.

Then there is psychic surgery but without the healer entering the body physically. The healer is literally psychic and can see into the body. They are able to watch the healing energy at work. This is what I do by channelling my Chinese doctor.

Channelling his words at the beginning of this chapter was interesting for me. It is now clear to me that surgeons in spirit work through all professional healers, but can only be seen when that healer is confident and strong enough to take the responsibility.

So really, developing your healing skills not only strengthens your ability to channel the energy, but also strengthens your ability to see what the problem is and to watch your guides at work.

I have lots of stories to tell of how my own doctor has worked through me. There is never any blood, never any need to enter the body. The only difference I can pick up is that as soon as my doctor appears and starts work, without my client even knowing that he is there, they all say that they can feel discomfort or intense pressure in that particular area. They know I am not even touching them, that my hands are several inches above them, but they feel like I am touching inside their body.

I now know the time it has taken to get to the stage where I am seeing this man at work, has been for me to learn to trust the energy running through me. All healers go through stages of disbelief and lack of confidence.

When a healer is completely and utterly trusting of the energy, with no doubt whatsoever that healing does heal, they will be ready to see.

Chapter 13

Remove the ego.

Ego is something that is beyond belief. So many of you truly believe that it is you performing the surgery. This is yet another block for us to work through.

Please remember that healing is a natural talent, given to all beings. You need to be the channel for us to work through - nothing more.

Indeed you may have high spirits after we have completed our surgery, we take great pride in our work and feel contentment afterwards too, but give thanks to our Creator and be done.

Rhiannon shows excitement that I have learnt to contend with. Amusing as it is now, at first I could not accept this. The use of language these days is very different to us and traditions have certainly changed over the years. Connecting with you is always a pleasure but a learning curve for each involved.

Interesting hey? The excitement and satisfaction that we feel after giving a healing session is normal. I am blown away with the things I am privy to seeing. I feel honoured to be a part of it. However, I am fully aware that it is not me doing it. I come home to my husband who dutifully asks if I have had a good day, and tell him what I saw my guides do - I never come home saying what amazing things I have done.

The excitement the doc has embarrassingly mentioned that I show, comes through shock I think! Having been surrounded by people in my life who laugh at the idea of healing, clairvoyance and tarot, I am passionate about my work and just gob smacked and delighted at the things I witness. In this horrible world, filled with man made disasters, I see it as constant proof to me that God exists and we are just one small world, part of a very large collection of worlds who should all be working together in peace and harmony.

To All Healers, With Love from a Healer

Chapter 14

Removing negative energy

I do not assist Rhiannon with this area of her work. It is an essential part of her duty and she is protected by Viala and many other entities. This can be an important part of healing as a preventative to serious ill health.

Well, I learnt something new there, I didn't know the name of my guide who assists me with RNE. All I see is a huge man that I have named Watson. He looks a bit like Phil Mitchell off Eastenders - a big man, wearing a black bomber jacket. He walks right behind me when I go to someone's house to clear an energy. I like to think of him as my bodyguard.

Now, if I see him I realise that within the next five minutes I will either go to or meet a negative energy.

I have done a lot of house clearings and he appears instantly. Once I was going to give a Reiki session to a pregnant woman in her home, when I saw Watson waiting for me whilst I found my car keys. I thought to myself that it was odd that he was there and then started to get nervous.

Sure enough when I arrived at the woman's house, I felt a horrible energy instantly and the husband told me that they had no end of problems as someone had hung themselves many years ago at the top of their stairs. From that day on, I trusted the fact that every time I needed protection from Watson, I have it without even having to ask for it.

Removing negative energies from a person is just the same as removing it from a house or building.

It is a necessary part of healing someone. A negative energy is purely a spirit or soul that needs help. Some people call it rescue work. At the start of a healing session, sometimes you just can't get through - it feels like there is a black cloud around the person.

This is the first sign that tells me instantly that there is a negative energy around them. So firstly, what is it ? It is nothing to be afraid of, as the golden rule is good always beats bad.

A negative energy could be someone in spirit, whether they knew the person or not, who is trying to influence or live their life through your customer. Why would they do this? Because they have unfinished business, they died suddenly without achieving everything they wanted or needed to do. Or maybe because they are concerned about your customer's life and they are only trying to help.

If I died tomorrow, I would be classed as a negative energy to my children, as there is no way I would just sit back and watch them make mistakes in their life. I would still want to be involved and be the bossy or pushy mother that I am today ! But this is not allowed, as we all have control of our own lives and destiny. We have to learn from our own mistakes. So many times, people listen to spirit as if their word is gospel. This is not the case! It is just their opinion the same as we all have. It does not make what they are saying right.

When we remove them, we are not banishing them, or hurting them. In actual fact we are helping them. We are just stopping them from forcing their thoughts or opinions onto us.

In other instances, a negative energy is someone who is desperately trying to get your attention and needs your help. Don't ever think of it as being a bad person. It doesn't matter if they were a mass murderer in their lifetime: they need your help to get them over to the light, or heaven.

It is a common problem of people who have

committed suicide. From what I have seen and experienced, when you commit suicide you do not go to "heaven" or spirit world. You are stuck in a very lonely place, almost stuck between the two worlds. Some people call this shadow land. The person needs your help to get them to the other side, the light or heaven, whatever you want to call it. This is where they will meet their guides and be loved and cared for.

Okay, so how do you remove a negative energy? This is the way.

Firstly,ask your guides to assist and protect you as always. Find the location where the energy has attached itself. Often you will find that it is a place where your customer already experiences problems, such as bad back, neck or hip etc.

You can find it by using your dowser or scanning the body with your hand. You will feel a cold sensation at the point where it has attached. Keep your hand over the area, and close your eyes. Say in your head, so as not to frighten your customer, the Lord's Prayer.

After that, visualise a door and open it with your mind's eye, to reveal a brilliant white light. Ask your guides to take the person through the door, where they will be safe and cared for.

"In love and light, I ask my guides to remove this negative energy"

I talk to the soul showing them the way to go and reassure them that they will be okay once through the door.

"Go through the light, we mean you no harm. You must leave this person alone and go through the door, where you will be safe and loved and cared for"

I watch them walk through the door and I always see their guides assist them. Once the door has been firmly closed, I say thank you to God.

Sometimes they need to tell me something before they go and I will always pass on the message. It will turn out to be closure for them. More often than not, they thank me for helping them and it can be a really emotional time.

Negative energies in houses are slightly different. This is because it is usually connected to the house rather than the person who is living in it. Maybe it is a previous owner who is not happy with who is living in their house now. Or sometimes, it is connected to the troubled ground that the house was built on. In these cases, I am not interested in finding out who it was, but I just use exactly the same routine as before and go around each and every room in the house and clear it with the use of a candle and incense.

I command them to leave and send them through the door, reassuring them that we mean them no harm but they are affecting the people living there now and must leave.

You may laugh, but I have seen children badly disturbed in their sleep, items moving around the house, bad smells appear when least expected and many frightening results of an unhappy 'ghost'.

Remember the golden rule, - good always beats bad. You are safe, protected and capable of removing anything.

It is always nice, to go back a few days later and see the difference. Negative energies can cause rifts in marriages, upset children, money problems - every part of your life can be affected and it doesn't have to be like that. It is easily removed and there is an instant difference in the family life afterwards.

You are using the same energy as you channel for healing - you are just healing a situation instead of a person.

Chapter 15

Teaching Reiki

Mastering levels of Reiki are no different to the young ones. We can work with all of you at different levels, however, we have to be sure you are ready to commit to such levels of healing. This is the reason why we refrain from coming in too soon.

Teachers of Reiki should also be practising in our opinion. There is no use preaching alone as all too soon the ego starts to show. Students start to look at you as the higher being, having all the knowledge, but this is not the case. Hands on practise and stories to tell of actual healing are what they need to hear.

Very true I say. How can you possibly teach somebody if you don't have regular hands on experience.

Notice he says that there is no difference between someone who has just passed their level I and a Reiki master? All too often, students become big headed after they have completed their training and can go no higher. They want to be as good as you , their teacher, just as qualified and capable. They look up to you and sometimes become in awe of you or your work. So the satisfaction when they have the same letters after their name as you can be dangerous. They stop learning.

The reality is that when you have your masters or whatever the top qualification is in your healing school, you have only just begun learning. You are fully equipped with all the tools you need, but experience is worth it's weight in gold. This only comes after some time working as a master.

I actually love teaching. It means I am busy every weekend as well as working full time in the shop in the week, but I learn something new from every single student I meet. I feel honoured that I am a part of their journey and I love meeting their guides and helping them join together as a partnership.

Never be afraid to turn a student away if you don't think they are ready for their spiritual journey. Sometimes, you just get a gut feeling that the person isn't ready yet. It also goes the other way too - maybe you are not the right teacher for them. Follow your intuition and ask for guidance when deciding whom to teach or who to be taught by.

Pricing up the courses is a tricky subject. You need to charge for your time and energy, just like when you give a session. Nobody expects you to do it for nothing. It also means that the person is serious about learning healing and is prepared to pay for it.

You will have had to create your own manuals, pay for paper, folders, heating electric etc for the room. Possibly even renting the room for the course. Look around at other Reiki course prices and try to stay at roughly the same price as most.

If you drop the price to a silly amount, you will be full with people who aren't really serious about the healing. If you raise the price well above competitors, you will be giving the impression that you are better or more experienced than other teachers. (Ego?)

Masters courses differ in price greatly. More false promises are given, trying to justify the amount they are asking for. Keep it to a realistic price, obviously much more than the other two levels, but still at a price that people can afford. Remember, we are aiming at the whole world benefiting from healing - not just the rich!

"A good teacher creates students who are better than him"

I was told this once and it makes a lot of sense to me now I am teaching. If you have done your job well, your students should be the best healers around. If you feel threatened by this, then you are teaching in the wrong way. A good teacher does not hold back on any information, hoping to be better than anyone. You have to pass on your skills and knowledge and know that your lineage is one to be proud of.

Once you start teaching, you will be aware of yet another guide working through you. He/She is the one who actually attunes the students. It is not uncommon for this person to be a Japanese master in Reiki, who once upon a time used to teach or perform on this earth plane.

I always come down with a bump after teaching. I feel my guide's presence so strongly whilst holding the classes and feel empty and small again after he has gone. My teaching guide is very tall, thin and serious man with an incredible grey beard. I have never been able to talk to him as he is busy working. I just watch in awe at the way he attunes the students. He always bows to me at the end before he leaves and I feel so honoured and grateful that he has chosen me.

I think the most important part of all my Reiki courses is showing students how to connect with their guides. Watching them learn to see and trust their guides is emotional for me. It is like match making or taking someone on a blind date! By the time the student is on their masters course, I am not needed. They just need the attunements from me and the rest is between them and their guides. It is important that you reassure your students that even though their journey has ended with you, as there are no more courses to do, you will always be there to help them. It is so sad when a teacher stops helping because no more money is being passed over !

What do you do if one of your students doesn't turn out the way you had hoped? What happens if one of your student's ego won't go away?
It will happen, you feel almost embarrassed that you are the one that taught them. Know that you

taught them in the same way as all the others and that you can only do your best to advise, but you can't make them listen.

In time, you will know before you take them on in the first place. As always ask your guides and follow your intuition. If you have a bad feeling about someone, then don't take them on !

You are never responsible for a student's actions after you have taught them. However, if you are a genuine person, you cannot help but feel bad if they falter. I find a good way of keeping them on the right track is staying in regular contact as a friend . Another good idea is to hold Reiki shares or open refresher sessions for fellow healers.

To All Healers, With Love from a Healer

Chapter 16

Why can't we heal everybody?

A person has to want to be healed.

I was waiting for a nice long paragraph to be dictated to me then. And all I got was that one sentence. After I had tried to call him back and ask him to carry on but with no response, I sat back and thought about it. I suddenly realised how much sense this one small sentence makes.

Customers who enjoy being ill.

Customers who enjoy the attention they get when they have problems.

Customers who absolutely refuse to take responsibility for their actions.

Customers who are angry and blame others for their misfortunes.

Customers who don't believe.

It sounds harsh, but it is true. People who are in a terrible relationship, physically or verbally beaten by another human being, have to first realise that they deserve better. Emotional healing will of course do the trick, heart chakra as we all know by now. But they need to feel self worth - which comes from within.

People who let their partners cheat on them and take them back over and over again, don't feel that they deserve happiness or love. For whatever reason, they are not wanting to deal with their underlying problem. Probably because it is too painful at the present moment. Isn't it better to be with someone than no-one? Self respect has to be achieved first.

People who are so lonely that the only attention

they get is when they are ill. They think that if they were fit and healthy, nobody would ask them how they are.

How about the non believers? Don't they just do your head in ? I spent so much time in the early days trying to convince people of my beliefs and show them how it can help or change their life. What's the point? They have to sincerely want the Reiki and sincerely get better, whether it's an emotional problem or a physical one.

Intent is needed to give Reiki as we have spoken about, but belief is needed to receive it too.

This does not relate to when it is a persons time to die. We all have a time to leave this life. It is hard as a healer, to realise you can't prevent it from happening. Healing will help though, making it more gentle and less distressing.

To All Healers, With Love from a Healer

About the Author

Rhiannon Faulkner lives in Devon with her husband Dave and her family. She has five young children and runs a company called Say It With Angels, where she teaches Tarot and Reiki healing. She gives private tarot readings, medium and healing sessions in her shop in Newton Abbot. Her reputation is growing, with clients travelling from all over the country for her readings and healing classes.

Rhiannon is also author of "My Journey Through The Tarot" and "The Faulkner Tarot Deck".

In her centre in Newton Abbot she offers the following:

1. Healing Sessions
2. Tarot Readings
3. Clairvoyancy
4. Tarot Courses
5.Reiki Courses I, II and Masters

See website: www.sayitwithangels.co.uk